Heinkel He 111

Written by Ron Mackay

Walk Around®

Squadron Signal® Publications

Cover Art by Don Greer

Line Illustrations by Melinda Turnage

(Front Cover) An Oslo-based He 111P is forced down by a Fleet Air Arm 'Skua' fighter during the 1940 Norwegian Campaign.

(Back Cover) KG26 was specifically allocated a torpedo-bombing role from 1941 and operated over the Arctic and Mediterranean. This 5 Staffel machine is depicted while serving in the latter-named Theater of Operations.

About the Walk Around® Series

The Walk Around® series is about the details of specific military equipment using color and black-and-white archival and photographs of in-service, preserved, and restored equipment. *Walk Around®* titles are devoted to aircraft and military vehicles. These are picture books focus on operational equipment, not one-off or experimental subjects.

Squadron/Signal Walk Around® books feature the best surviving and restored historic aircraft and vehicles. Inevitably, the requirements of preservation, restoration, exhibit, and continued use may affect these examples in some details of paint and equipment. Authors strive to highlight any feature that departs from original specifications.

Proudly printed in the U.S.A.
Copyright 2012 Squadron/Signal Publications
1115 Crowley Drive, Carrollton, TX 75006-1312 U.S.A.
www.SquadronSignalPublications.com

Hardcover ISBN 978-0-89747-693-5
Softcover ISBN 978-0-89747-694-2

Military/Combat Photographs and Snapshots

If you have any photos of aircraft, armor, soldiers, or ships of any nation, particularly wartime snapshots, please share them with us and help make Squadron/Signal's books all the more interesting and complete in the future. Any photograph sent to us will be copied and returned. Electronic images are preferred. The donor will be fully credited for any photos used. Please send them to the address above.

(Title Page) The He111P-2 prior to its inclusion in the Gardermoen Air Museum's collection still lacks landing gear doors for the port engine nacelle but is otherwise in its original external condition with markings for 4/KG4 with which it operated.

Acknowledgments

Lars-Kristian Iversen, the Gardermoen Museum Curator, earns my gratitude for his efforts in making the He111P-2 available. He trusted me and Olaf Aspen who arranged the visit to clamber in unrestricted but responsible fashion inside and around the aircraft. Pete Nash and his dedicated restoration team at the RAF Museum, Hendon, provided similar comprehensive facilities for the He111H-20 based there. Their technical advice proved equally invaluable and I thank them for this as well as their forbearance in granting unfettered access. Finally, the following individuals assisted with photographs of the He111 in service; Olaf Aspen, James V. Crow, Ed Dalrymple, and Jerry Scutts.

Introduction

The unwelcome wavering beat of the He 111's engines will ever be an iconic aural image of the Luftwaffe's nocturnal Blitz upon Britain as well as its presence over other European countries during WWII. Recruited by Ernst Heinkel in January 1931, the twin brothers Siegfried and Walter Günter designed the aircraft, which first flew in early 1935 and began service as a civil airliner. Soon, however, it was adapted to the more deadly role of a bomber. Despite its growing obsolescence as the conflict progressed, it was retained on front-line duties, mainly thanks to the Reichsluftfahrtministerium's (RLM's) failure to introduce new and superior performance designs, particularly in the strategic bombardment role – a thankful lapse, in terms of ultimate Allied victory.

The Heinkel 111 saw service on all Germany's military fronts in the European Theater of World War II. It began the war serving as a medium bomber, supporting German ground campaigns. After the Soviet Union and its western Allies acquired air superiority in 1943, the He 111 was largely relegated to its original transport functions. A few bomber units continued to employ the He 111 as a bomber, largely at night in order to avoid Allied fighters, until 1945.

In addition to its service with the German armed forces, the Heinkel 111 was also exported to a number of countries. Beginning in the 1930s, Turkey and China purchased 28 and 12 of the aircraft, respectively. German He 111s provided support for Francisco Franco's Nationalist army during the Spanish Civil War, after which Berlin gave 59 surviving aircraft to the Madrid dictator. Franco's Spain later acquired six more He 111s during the years of World War II. Germany's wartime partners Bulgaria, Romania, Hungary, and the rump state of Slovakia all also acquired a number of the aircraft.

The number of intact He 111 airframes available for examination is small and reflects almost the opposite ends of the design's production-range between 1939 and 1945. The P-2 variant that forms the bulk of this volume's contemporary content is a standard bomber that was assigned to Kampfgeschwader 4 (KG4) "General Wever." The staff of Gardermoen Museum, Oslo, have faithfully restored it to virtual original configuration prior to being fatally crippled by a Fleet Air Arm "Skua" and forced down onto Norwegian soil during the Nazi Invasion launched on 9 April 1940. A lack of landing gear doors and the absence of the various circular caps on the upper wing surfaces hardly detract from the overall high quality of restoration.

By contrast The RAF Museum's example, although externally in complete order, is a late-production H-20/R1 converted to transport duties and featuring a "solid" equipment support frame underneath in place of the bomb bay. In addition, the restoration procedure has not yet been applied to the cockpit section in particular. Nevertheless, the general external appearance of the He 111 is common to both variants while the internal layout of the P-2 would accord with that applied to the He 111H bomber variants.

I accordingly believe that the content of this book provides sound coverage of the He 111 in terms of the aviation modelling fraternity's search for accurately completed models. Several further pictures, although gleaned from post-War airframes, nevertheless provide details that accord with the WWII construction of the Heinkel design.

The inability of the He 111 to carry a bomb exceeding 250kgs internally is exemplified by this He 111H. An SC1000 high-explosive weapon is mounted on a PVC1006 rack positioned to one side of the aircraft's centerline.

A view of the He 111P-2 from a frontal angle accentuates the slim lines of the fuselage and the continuous top-line of the cockpit area, as well as the equally slim lines of the DB 601 engine cowlings.

The P-variant of the Heinkel design introduced the Ikaria rotating nose panel that was offset to starboard. This was done in order to provide the pilot sitting on the port-side with a clearer forward view.

A mix of optically flat Plexiglas panels are fitted to the lower cockpit section in the forward nose area. The streamlined "periscope" structure that extends below the nose usually accommodates the Lotfernrohr 7C ("Lotfe 7C") bomb-sight.

The outlines of the pair of bottom-hinged blanked-out frames are visible in the center right of the P-2's fuselage. When lowered, these frames provide access to the top of the bomb bay. Another pair of frames are located on the port side of the fuselage.

The Gardermoen P-2 was assigned to Kampfgeschwader (KG) 4 that bore the title of "General Wever." The 5J part of the code denotes the Geschwader. The aircraft flew with the 5th Staffel as confirmed by the Black N. The aircraft-letter C is Red, the color assigned to each Gruppe's second Staffel, confirming that this P-2 flew with II/KG4

Due to the severe punishment inflicted during the Battle of Britain, the original three-gun armament complement was supplemented. In this case machine-guns were mounted in the rear fuselage windows. The circular gun-mount frame is screwed into the Plexiglas. The T-pattern metal frame is mounted onto the fuselage structure.

The rear pair of window frames are positioned on both sides of the radio compartment, which is located directly behind the bomb bay. The frames' rectangular shape with rounded corners was a design feature common to the majority of He 111 variants.

The small inset circle with a bar across the middle is positioned below the rear window and is one of several such securing points for a tarpaulin to cover the aircraft on the ground in inclement weather. The hand-painted white lettering on this aircraft is misspelled and presumably dates to some time after the war. *Zur Öse für Plane* (meaning "Securing point for tarpaulin") are presumably the intended words.

The large panel directly above the pilot's seat can be slid back along the raised metal runner frames visible behind the panel.

The small panel directly ahead of the sliding panel is a flexible unit hinged at the forward edge. When raised into position it acts as a windshield for the pilot. The dark shape ahead of the red container is an ammunition drum that is housed in a frame mounted in the cockpit roof.

When the pilot slid back this sliding panel (seen here from a forward, oblique angle) and elevated his seat, he could gain a better view, particularly in rain or heavy cloud conditions when visibility through the cockpit Plexiglas was correspondingly poor.

The He 111's cockpit is provided with sliding side window panels. These are located directly below the forward section of the cockpit sliding panel, and are level with the pilot's seat.

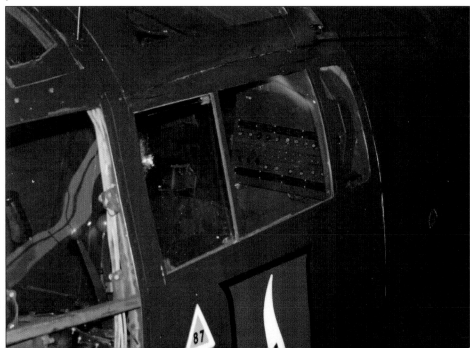

The large shield is the KG4 "General Wever" insignia. Overall color is Red with a Black outline. The Black symbol in the center has a wavy White background. The 87 within the yellow/white triangle denotes the engine fuel's octane strength. The manufacturer's plate on the He 111 is located forward of the shield's base-line.

The He 111's distinctive Ikaria GD-A 1114 rotating gun-mount is seen from the outside. The mount can be rotated and in the case of the P-2 variant is equipped with a 7.92mm MG 15 machine-gun. Later He 111 variants carried a 13mm MG 131 machine gun or an MG FF 20mm cannon.

The He 111's bomb-sight is housed above an external oval-shaped "periscope" with a rectangular aperture through which the sight is focused. The optically-flat panel alongside the "periscope's" right-side is hinged on the right and opens outwards.

The connection point for starting up the He 111 using a trolley accumulator is positioned just behind the lower cockpit Plexiglas and to starboard of the fuselage center-line. The wording stencilled in red is a post-war addition and *Elektr. Aussenbord Anschluss,* meaning "external electrical connection," is the inscription.

The port-side lower fuselage securing eye for tarpaulins is located just ahead of the bomb bay and inner fuel-tank panel. Surrounding the securing eye is red painted lettering, which is spelled incorrectly and was evidently crudely applied to the aircraft in the course of restoration. Presumably the intended words are *Zur Öse für Plane*.

The P-2's Ikaria gun-mount is seen from the inside. Small frame at the top right is the housing for a flare-signal pistol. The optically flat panels extend further up on the port side compared to the starboard-side of the cockpit nose area.

The orange container forward of the radio compass normally holds the flares for the signal pistol. Two spare ammunition drums are located in a floor clip and on the cockpit roof.

This is an overall view of the P-2's forward cockpit area. The pilot's view via the curved Plexiglas panels was liable to be badly restricted in poor weather or in bright sunlight conditions. The recommended overall color for Luftwaffe cockpit interiors was RLM66 Black-Gray, which officially replaced RLM02 Gray around 1939/1940.

Nose Development

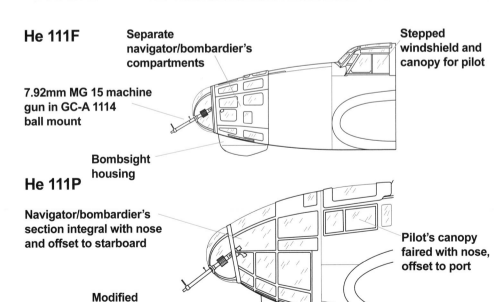

He 111F

Separate navigator/bombardier's compartments

Stepped windshield and canopy for pilot

7.92mm MG 15 machine gun in GC-A 1114 ball mount

Bombsight housing

He 111P

Navigator/bombardier's section integral with nose and offset to starboard

Pilot's canopy faired with nose, offset to port

Modified bombsight housing

The black cover on the cockpit floor directly behind the Ikaria gun-mount covers up the Bombenschütze's (Bombardier's) frame. Other points of note are the pilot's U-pattern handgrips on the control column extension arm and the cylinder below the pilot's seat that is part of the bellows system for raising the seat.

The He 111's control-column is offset to the right of the pilot's seat. The hand-grips are attached to a flexible extension-arm that swings over to the right for other crewmembers to use in an emergency. The "inverted L" lever behind the left foot-pedal along with the same fitting on the right-hand pedal is used to elevate the pilot's seat.

A clock is mounted on the pilot's control column and anti-slip metal inserts are positioned on the front of the pilot's black hand grips. Not present on this restored aircraft is a three-position turn switch normally mounted on the top of the right hand-grip. This switch would operate the automatic pilot system that applies only to the rudder. The square unit with the word *Ruf* ("call") is the pilot's intercom control box.

The Gray rudder pedals on the He 111 extend out over the lower-cockpit Plexiglas. They are shaped to fit the pilot's flying boots with a raised rim at the rear and are also equipped with leather toe-loops.

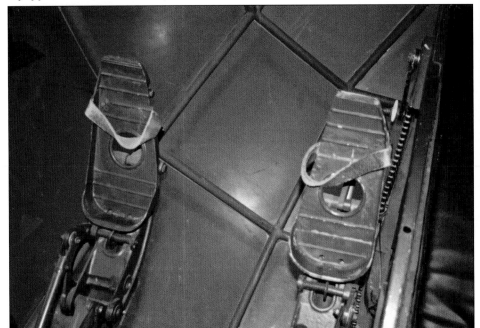

A view of the control column from behind picks out the hexagonal securing nut for the extension arm and the securing clips for the pilot's intercom control box. The control column frame is finished overall in RLM02 Gray.

11

The primary instrument panel for the pilot of the He 111P-2 is mounted in the cockpit ceiling. The panel appears to be finished in RLM02 Gray although RLM66 Black-Gray was supplanting the Gray around the time of this aircraft's service.

The course-setting frame is located to the right-front of the pilot's seat. Red wording advises the operator to place the counter at top left and the large lever on the left in a zero position before engaging and disengaging the equipment. Morse-code variations recorded on either side of the small panel at bottom left tells the pilot when he is straying either side of the constant tone signal that indicates the selected course.

The right side of the panel holds the engine-monitoring dials. At the top left are the engine revolution counter units with the boost pressure gauges below. Oil and coolant temperature gauges are top and bottom-center respectively. All dials are black-rimmed except for the coolant temperature frames, which are Red.

A second set of instrument dials is contained in a metal frame placed centrally in the cockpit roof. The left-hand pair of dial frames house the fuel contents gauges, with the fuel selector switches on either side. The right-hand pair of dials is believed to be the oil/fuel pressure gauges. Dial rims are painted yellow.

The artificial horizon is mounted at the extreme left of the panel with (L-R) the turn-and-bank, rate-of-climb, and altimeter dials. The repeater compass is in the center of the panel with the directional gyro below. The two dials in line with the compass are (L-R) the blind-approach and airspeed indicators.

The red handle attached to the right side of the instrument box on the ceiling is the emergency release for the bomb bay. The red-painted metal loop is the lever for opening the large Plexiglas panel. The word *Notausgang* on the lever translates as "emergency exit."

Another panel to the front-left of the pilot's seat contains the propellers' pitch-angle dials (top). Flap and landing gear position-indicator dials are bottom left and right. The large black dial monitors the aircraft's climb/descent-rate.

The engine and propeller controls for the He 111 are mounted into a second box-frame that is positioned in an angled-up attitude to the left of the pilot's seat. The oxygen apparatus container is positioned below the frame front.

13

He 111B-1 Specifications

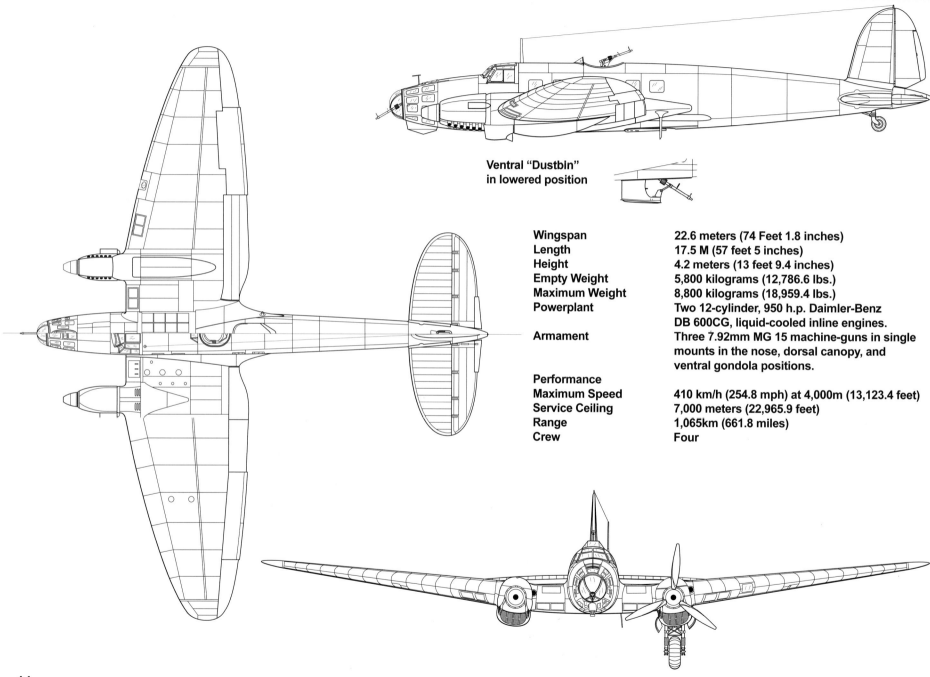

**Ventral "Dustbin"
in lowered position**

Wingspan	22.6 meters (74 Feet 1.8 inches)
Length	17.5 M (57 feet 5 inches)
Height	4.2 meters (13 feet 9.4 inches)
Empty Weight	5,800 kilograms (12,786.6 lbs.)
Maximum Weight	8,800 kilograms (18,959.4 lbs.)
Powerplant	Two 12-cylinder, 950 h.p. Daimler-Benz DB 600CG, liquid-cooled inline engines.
Armament	Three 7.92mm MG 15 machine-guns in single mounts in the nose, dorsal canopy, and ventral gondola positions.
Performance	
Maximum Speed	410 km/h (254.8 mph) at 4,000m (13,123.4 feet)
Service Ceiling	7,000 meters (22,965.9 feet)
Range	1,065km (661.8 miles)
Crew	Four

This is the example of the He 111P-2 variant that was shot down over Norway during the Nazi Invasion of that country in April 1940. The aircraft was recovered from the crash-site in 1976 and painstakingly restored to this condition over a period of six years. The work took place at Gardermoen Museum outside Oslo where the bomber is also displayed.

Green T-pattern handles on large frame by the pilot's seat control the engine radiator movements. The orange handle behind operates the landing gear/flap emergency systems. Yellow levers are fuel-system primers and (left-side) fuel-transfer control.

The two engine throttle levers are located at the front of the engine control box frame. The ball-pattern tops on the levers are orange in color. The box frame appears sprayed overall in RLM02 Gray.

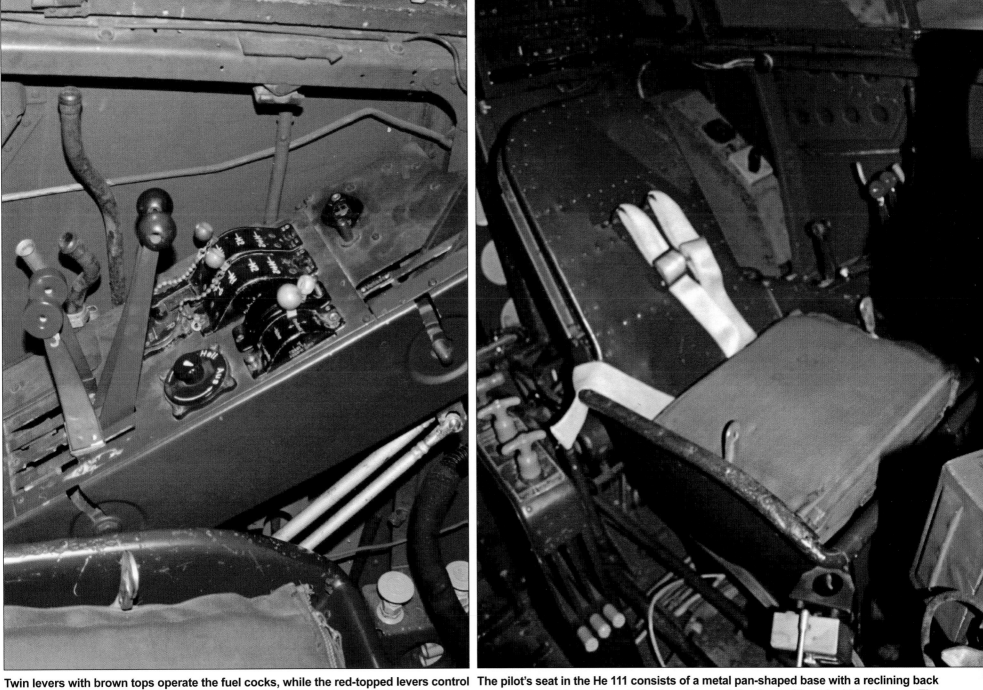

Twin levers with brown tops operate the fuel cocks, while the red-topped levers control the engine superchargers. The semi-circular black unit on the frame's left side has small levers that control the pitch of the propellers, while the fuel tank selector levers are positioned within the right-hand curved black unit.

The pilot's seat in the He 111 consists of a metal pan-shaped base with a reclining back support. A cushion with a zip for inserting padding is positioned within the pan. The elevator trim-wheel, normally positioned on the seat's right side, is absent. The snap-hooks attached to the seat secure the pilot's harness straps.

The top row of the electrical control panel buttons monitor (L-R) airscrew-pitch gear, the landing gear horn, aircraft's trim, temperature and content gauges, fuel transfer pump, directional gyro, course motor, course magnet, and the economical flight switch.

The bottom row monitors (L-R) radio systems, starboard and port generator (With a remote-controlled main switch in between), detachable and bomb armament, and the distribution switch for lights and pilot's heating.

The pilot's seat can be elevated whenever bad weather is encountered that restricts forward visibility and forces him to fly with his head out in the open. The seat-elevation bellows mechanism is linked to a rectangular retention structure by heavy-duty spindles.

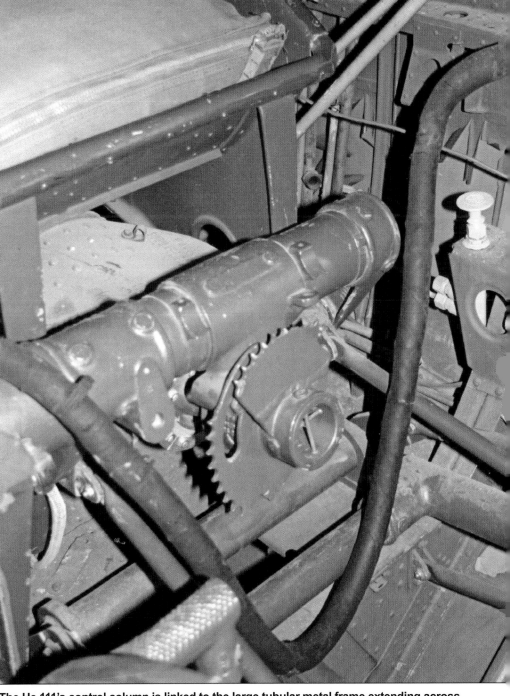

The oxygen apparatus for the pilot is contained in a frame fitted to the lower cockpit side. The frame is white and the lower section of the apparatus is in an orange cover. The yellow-painted unit below the apparatus allows the pilot to prime the engine cylinders.

The He 111's control column is linked to the large tubular metal frame extending across the base of the pilot's seat. Also seen is a vertically-aligned semi-circular frame with serrated edges that appears to be part of the seat-elevation mechanism.

The He 111's navigator is provided with a collapsible seat that is secured to the cockpit side, level with the pilot's seat. The frame appears to be sprayed in RLM66 Black-Gray. The absence of a fixed or flexible desk-top must have added to his problems on longer-range sorties.

The He 111's "Patin" radio-compass is positioned ahead of the navigator's seat. The circular frame is white and is secured to the inverted-U tubular support by four hexagonal nuts. The deviation indicator is seen at the base. The handle underneath operates the D/F loop aerial.

The He 111's bomb-bay layout was unique in that the ESAC/250IX racks were vertically aligned, as distinct from the horizontally-aligned bomb bays on other World War II bombers. There are four racks on either side of the bomb bay, each with a maximum bomb-weight capacity of 250kgs

The bombs are loaded nose-upwards, and the circular mountings in the bay roof, each aligned with a rack, are probably the connectors for the release mechanism leads. The title ESAC *(Elektrische senkrecht Aufhängung für Cylindrischebomben)* translates as "electrically-activated vertical bomb-rack."

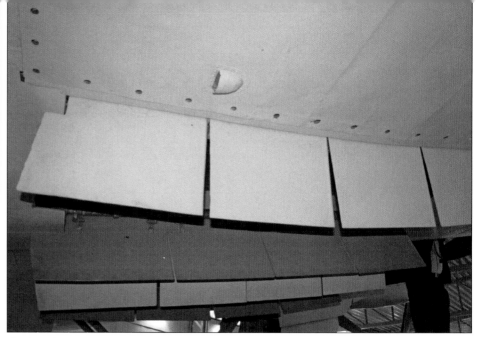

The navigator's seat is now seen in the deployed position. The simple structure with its semi-circular frame and T-pattern canvas back support must have provided a minimum of comfort when flying on lengthy missions.

A close-up of the door-operating mechanism shows how each sub-unit is attached to its tubular control rod by supports at either end. The small recess at the inner-rear face of the door is repeated on the other three rear doors.

The bomb-bay doors on the He 111 feature another variation on standard designs. They each consist of four separate units as opposed to a single continuous length. The outer doors flank the wings' inner fuel tank panels that are secured by large screw-nuts.

This is an overall frontal view of the He 111's bomb bay. Missing from the front of each bay is the "barred" grill, which was deployed to act as a slipstream spoiler, so preventing the airflow from disturbing the bombs' trajectory as they emerged from their racks.

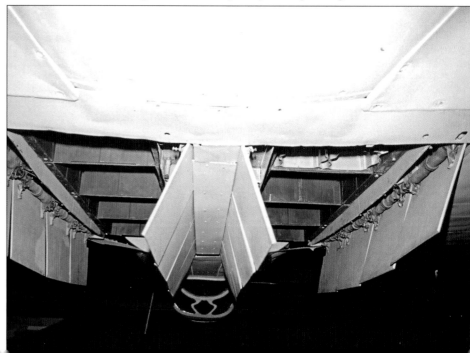

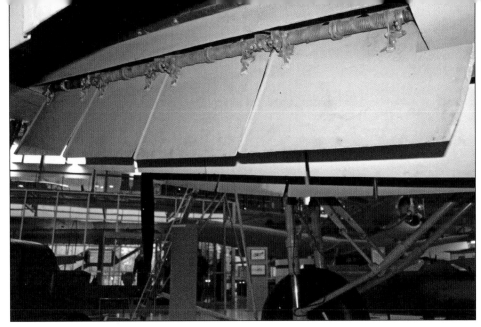

Tubular metal rods operate the bomb-bay doors. The inner edge of each forward door features a cutout with larger recesses on the inside sub-units as seen here. The spaces created by that design permitted the deployment of the "barred" grilles when the bomb-bay doors were opened.

The He 111's bomb-bay doors were angled slightly inwards even when fully opened as is evident in this picture. Flexibility of the doors permitted their safe deflection on occasions when the bomb-load was released prior to the doors' being in the fully open position.

A view of the left-front bomb-rack shows its sub-division into four cells in order to accommodate SC50 bombs or incendiary containers. Cables mounted in the bomb bay were attached to the bomb-noses for hoisting them up.

Bomb Bay Door "Barred" Grille

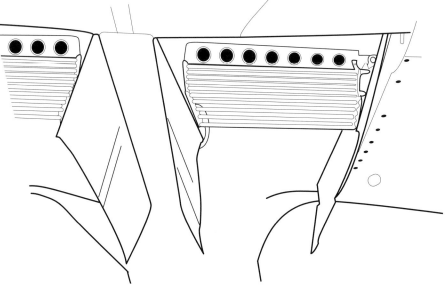

A full upward view of one of the other seven bomb racks demonstrates its stark simplicity. The automatic consecutive-release of each rack's content was made using an RAB 14z mechanism that was introduced into operational service on the He 111P variant. The telescopic fuse-charging arms extended downward to be attached to the bomb's circular fuse-base or bases. (Some SC250s were fitted with two fuses).

In the front section of the radio operator/gunner's compartment, the main communications equipment is mounted onto the forward left-side of the fuselage and the ceiling. At the top-center in this image is the gunner's seat-frame.

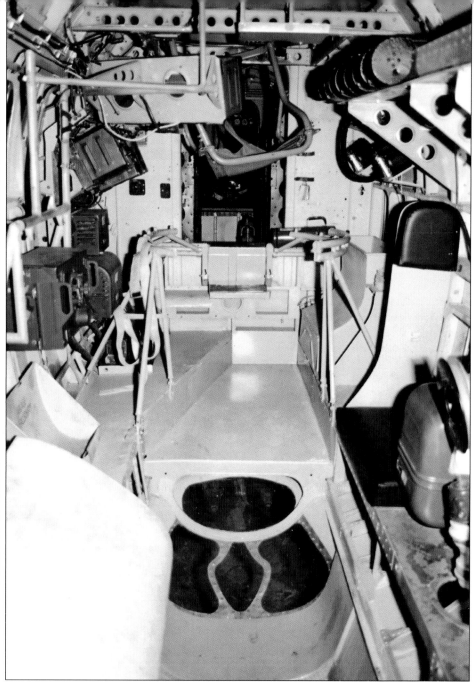

This is a general view of the radio operator/gunner's compartment directly behind the He 111's bomb bay. The radio equipment is positioned at the left-front of the compartment. Also seen is the gunner's seat-frame suspended from the forward section of the compartment ceiling.

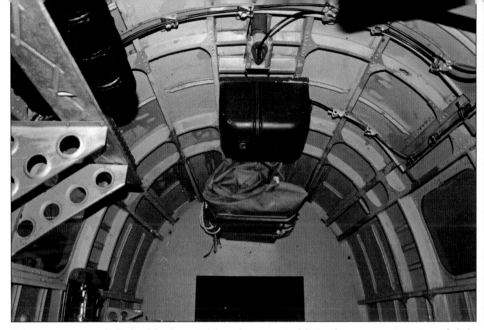

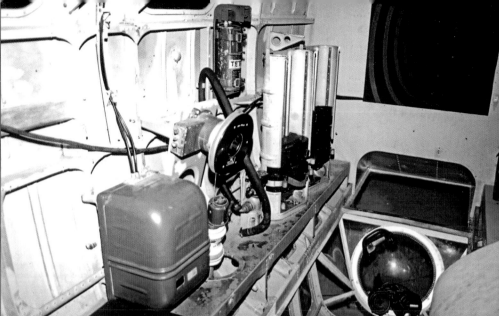

A large power-unit in its black metal box is mounted into the compartment roof. It is positioned directly behind the radio-mast, whose black wiring-lead is seen feeding out of the slot at the base.

The crew's life-raft is located at the rear of the compartment. It is secured to a wooden frame that is secured to the compartment roof by four corner-mounted straps. There is no hatch outline directly above; an external dinghy hatch on the He 111H variant was positioned directly behind the bulkhead, giving access to the rear fuselage.

The starboard-rear area of the radio compartment is occupied at the back by two vertical ammunition drum containers, with the trailing-aerial equipment directly ahead. Also seen is the square access hatch to the rear fuselage. The containers are sprayed white.

The radio trailing aerial equipment is positioned directly ahead of the ammunition containers. The aerial wire is wound round the black wheel-frame and extends downwards. The wire is threaded through a black-topped and white-base fitting fed into a fairing whose top can be seen within the circular cut-out in the support frame.

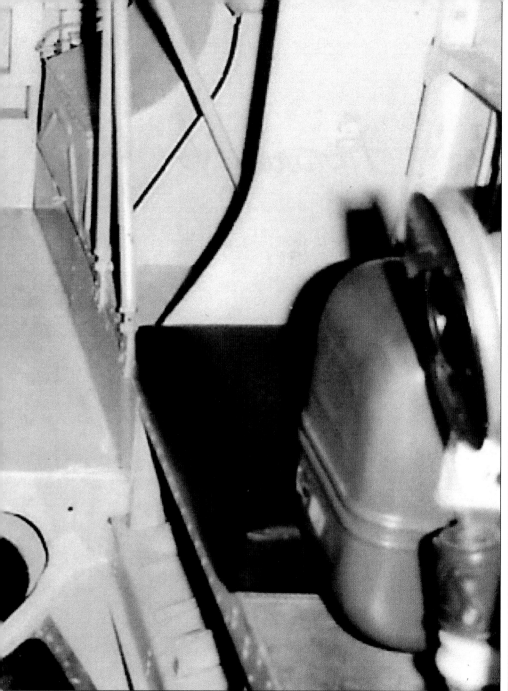

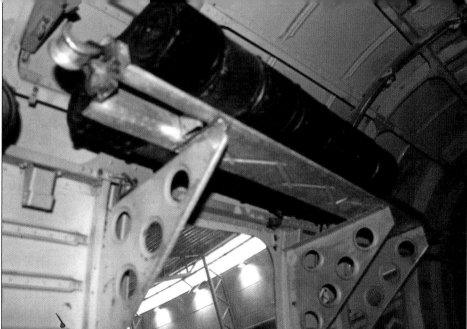

A storage shelf is positioned above the compartment windows on the starboard side. The shelf has capacity for seven ammunition drums and is held up by three triangular frames, each possessing five lightening holes.

This is a closer view of the ammunition drum containers. Each is cut back towards the base to allow the gunner to slide the bottom drum out. Red-sprayed clamps are fitted at the top and bottom

The forward end of the frame supporting the ammunition drum container and trailing-aerial equipment has a vertical section to which a head-rest is fitted. A cushion is also positioned on the support frame. RLM66 Black-Gray appears to be the head-rest color.

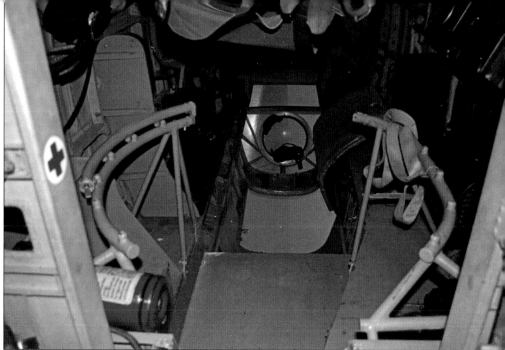

The gunner's seat in the radio compartment consists of a tubular metal frame. The rear corners are attached directly to the turret's circular base; the front frame-ends are linked to thin metal rods that extend forward to the circular base. The canvas seating and back-support straps are light tan with thin red center lines.

Just ahead of the shelf are four support units for ammunition drums. Tan leather straps secure the black drums in place. An oxygen flask and rubber tube are in the center.

A view of the radio compartment looking back from the rear of the bomb bay. Tubular metal frames are positioned on either side of the walk-way. The crew access hatch is opened up on the compartment's port-side.

A second view of the gunner's seat reveals how the back of the frame supports have metal loops attached using clamps at each end. The bases of these loops are fitted with small U-pattern brackets.

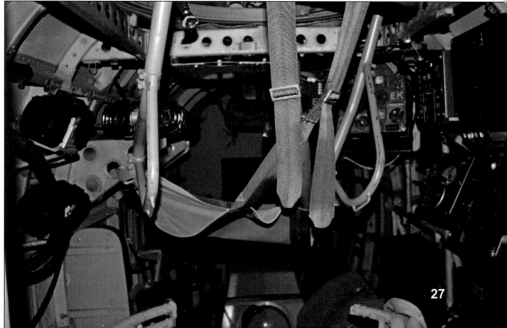

The He 111's radio-system boxes are located at the front-left of the compartment. The two seen here are the long-wave (L) and short-wave (R) units. The letters SL and SK on the exterior denotes *Sender-Langwelle* and *Sender-Kurzwelle* respectively.

The Radio-operator's control box on left has a large dial with a lever switch. Blue color segments relate to long-range transmitter/receiver operations and red to short-range operations. The tuning control is at top left.

The radio-receiver units are suspended at an angle to the transmitters, using an inverted-L Tubular frame that is secured to the left fuselage side. The letters EL and EK embossed on the exterior of the boxes denote Empfänger-Langwelle (Long-range receiver) and Empfänger-Kurzwelle (Short-wave receiver) respectively.

The box unit directly above the control set contains various switches, both for internal and external communications. Box units are finished in RLM74 Dark Gray.

What appears to be an auxiliary power unit (APU) is located on the compartment floor underneath the transmission boxes.

Above the stowage bin is a rectangular frame with a selector switch left of center. The frame, whose flexible cover is held in place by spring-clips, is clamped to the inverted-U tubular piping. Lift handles are fitted for transporting the frame.

A parachute stowage bin is positioned directly ahead of the front of the entrance hatch, which can be seen to the left in the open position.

A large square aperture in the top-center of the rear bulkhead provides access to the rear fuselage of the He 111. The P-2 variant at Gardermoen lacks the control cables for operation of the rudder and elevators.

The clean lines of the He 111 airframe are exemplified by the low, streamlined profile of the Plexiglas cover for the dorsal gunner. The cover can slide along the metal runner at its base. It also protects the gunner from the slipstream-blast to which he was subject in the open dorsal turrets of earlier He 111 versions.

A less angular view of the dorsal turret cover picks out the direction finder, which is located directly behind the gunner's position. On the He 111P-1, the D/F loop had been externally-mounted behind the dorsal turret. The unit is dark red in color.

Dorsal Gun Position Development

He 111F

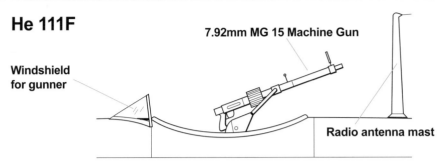

Windshield for gunner

7.92mm MG 15 Machine Gun

Radio antenna mast

He 111P

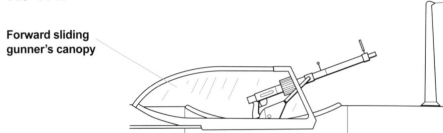

Forward sliding gunner's canopy

Dorsal Armament Development

He 111H-16

13mm MG 131 in fixed canopy

He 111H-21

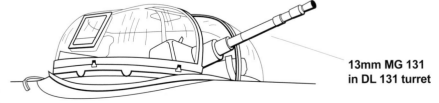

13mm MG 131 in DL 131 turret

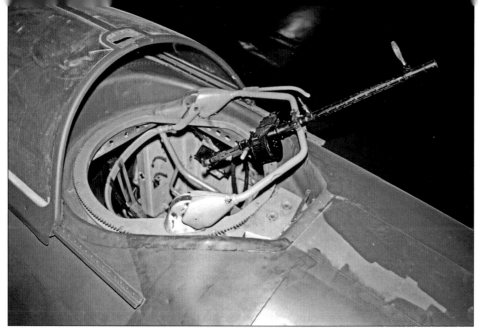

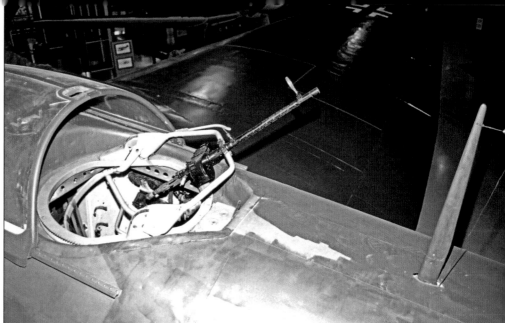

An overall view of the dorsal turret picks out the flexible frame to which an MG 15 7.92mm machine gun is attached. This neat, slim-lined weapon was the standard means of defence for Luftwaffe bombers at the beginning of WWII.

The flared triangular ends of the gun-mounting frame swivel on curved fittings that are mounted on the rim of the turret ring. The gunner's seat frame is linked to the inside surfaces of the gun-mounting frame. The centrally located handgrip, used to move the Plexiglas cover back and forth, is rimmed with wood.

The He 111P-2's radio mast is placed behind the dorsal turret. It is vertically tapered almost to its base when it assumes a parallel pattern. The horizontal aerial wire is secured to the aerial through a small eyelet. The vertical wire feeds into the 'teardrop' recess in the fuselage.

This close-up view of the dorsal turret's MG 15 picks out the weapon's securing clamp in the middle of the flexible frame. The rear section of the machine-gun lacks its circular cover.

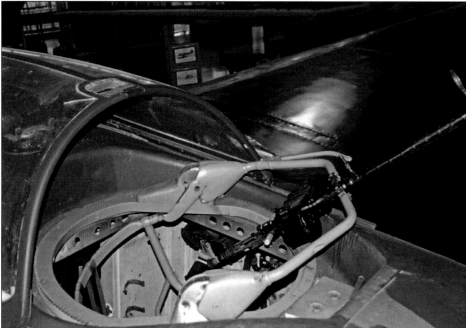

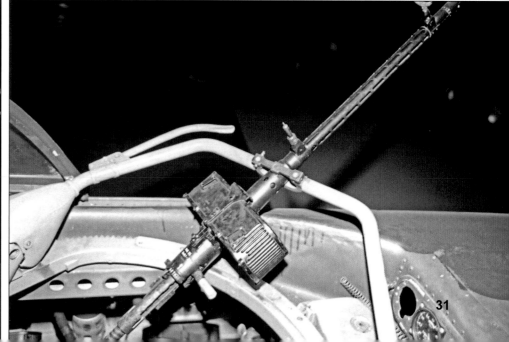

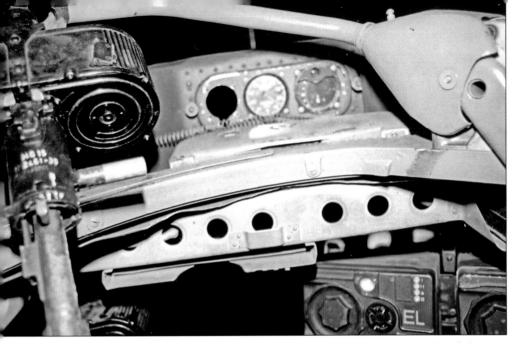

Three repeater instrument dials were originally mounted on the port side of the rear turret lip. The clock is missing from the left-hand mount, but the other two mounts contain an altimeter (center) and blind approach indicator

This P-2's individual aircraft letter, stencilled in black onto the top of the fuselage center-line, appears here in a view looking forward over the top of the dorsal turret Plexiglas. Stencilling the letter in this location was not a standard procedure.

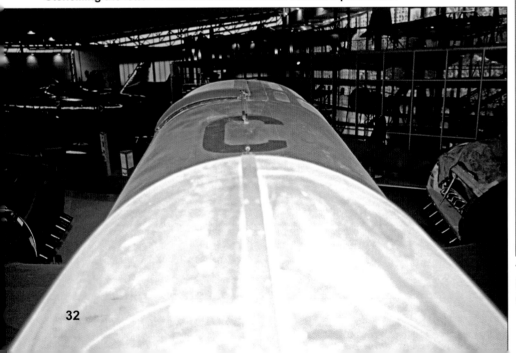

The fin and rudder of the He 111 feature an overall curved outline. The rudder sub-unit is almost as large as the fin. The entire surface is metal-skinned. The Werk Nummer (Aircraft's serial number) is stencilled in white at the top of the fin.

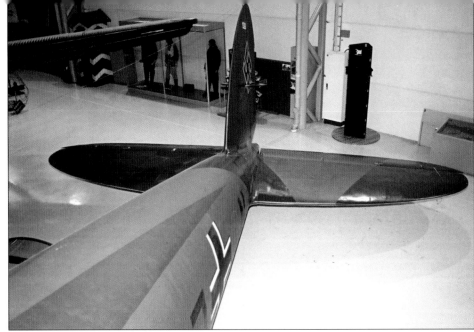

The view aft from the dorsal turret area reveals the continuing slim and streamlined nature of the He 111 fuselage. Also shown particularly in the foreground is the splinter-type camouflage with RLM70 Schwarzgrün (Black-Green) as the darker shade compared to the Dunkelgrün (Dark Green) shade

A lateral view of the He 111's tail structure emphasises both the size and the elliptical pattern of the vertical and horizontal control surfaces.

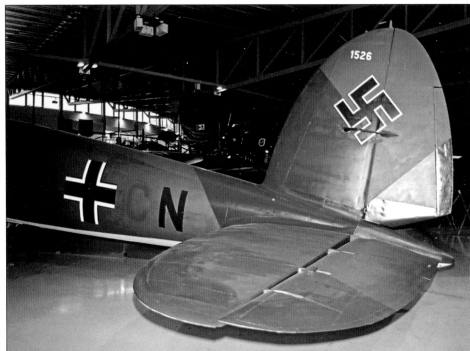

A closer view of the He 111's rudder demonstrates the neat manner in which its leading edge is faired into the rear of the fin surface. The rudder trim-tab is also sizeable in length, extending upwards in line with the seventh of the nine ribs forming the rudder's basic structure.

33

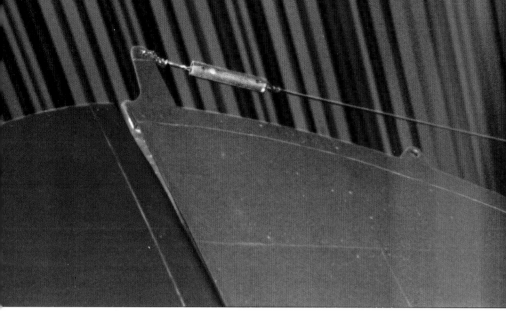

A vertical tab at the rear-top of the He 111's fin serves as an anchorage point for the main aerial wire. The smaller perforated triangular fitting, located further along the fin's top edge is a second aerial anchorage point for a second vertically-aligned wire to link up with the main wire, but it is not utilised in the preserved P-2's case.

The He 111P-2's rudder mass balance is seen here. The rear section is straight and is mounted into a triangular fairing. The forward section is curved and enters the fin through circular apertures. The mass balance patterns on H models were simpler in design

The He 111's rudder trim-tab frame contains seven ribs, and the forward edge slots neatly into the rudder. The actuating rod for the tab is located on the right side. White wording translates as "Do not touch!"

The rudder trim-tab is controlled by a single crank-shaped rod positioned on the starboard side. The forward end enters the rudder via a narrow channel inset into the central surface. This is a standard fitting on all He 111 variants.

Pitot Mast

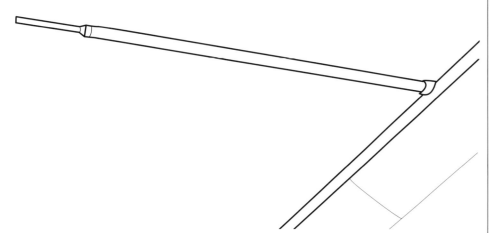

The horizontal stabilizer and elevator outline on the He 111 has a similar rounded pattern to the fin and rudder. The stabilizer possesses a single spar intersected by four inner lightweight frame-ribs and three solid outer ribs. The surfaces are metal-skinned. Tailplane adjustment through 3.2 degrees could be made manually.

There are 13 small scoop-pattern mountings facing to the rear on the rear edges of the stabilizers on both top and bottom surfaces. Three are seen here but their exact function is unclear. The flush-fitted elevator hinges are secured in place by hexagonal bolts.

The impression of slimness expressed by the He 111's fuselage shape is only marginally marred by the presence of the rudder mass-balance frame. Each elevator trim-tab extends to a point just inboard of a line with the second elevator hinge. The trim-tab control rods are not fitted.

The He 111's elevator frame consists of a single spar positioned towards the forward edge. It is intersected by seven ribs, the three outer solid-framed, the other four formed of top and bottom strips with Z-pattern framing in between. It is retained in position and activated by four "set-back" hinges. The red block across one hinge is a locking device to hold the elevator in place for purposes of museum display.

The He 111P-2's rear fuselage features an enclosed tail cone extending just beyond the line of the rudder. A number of He 111s were adapted to carry a machine-gun in this sub-unit. The elevator trim-tabs bear the same warning in white as the rudder trim-tab. Also seen is the angled cut-out in the base of the rudder

Large fairings are applied over the junction of the stabilizers with the fuselage. These comprise a single length with the raised semi-circular top edge in line with the stabilizer main spar.

The vertical fin and horizontal stabilizer are secured to the fuselage by pairs of heavy-duty bolts. These are positioned in rectangular recesses, in the case of the stabilizer/fuselage link above and below. Fairing strips have been detached from both sets of mountings in this instance.

Early Tail Gun

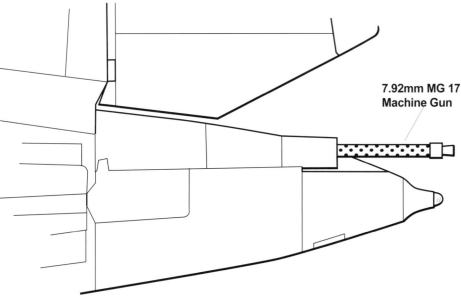

7.92mm MG 17
Machine Gun

Single length fairings are also applied to the junction of the fin with the fuselage. The fairings taper slightly outwards in a rearward direction.

The gondola fitting was introduced on the He 111P and initially held a single MG 15 at the rear. Single or twin guns were subsequently added at the forward end.

Ventral Gun Position Development

He 111F

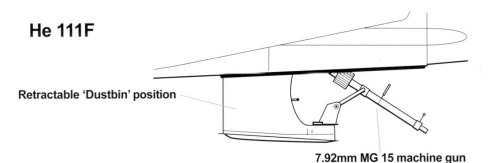

Retractable 'Dustbin' position

7.92mm MG 15 machine gun

He 111P

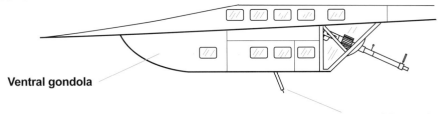

Ventral gondola

Radio antenna (Mounted on starboard side)

Ventral Armament Development

He 111H-6 (port side)

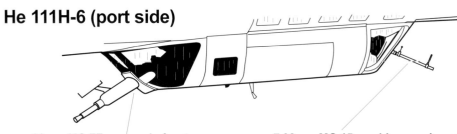

20mm MG FF cannon in front

7.92mm MG 15 machine gun in rear

He 111H-10/11 (starboard side)

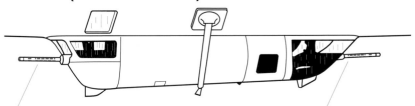

7.92mm MG 81Z machine gun in rear

13mm MG 131 machine gun in front

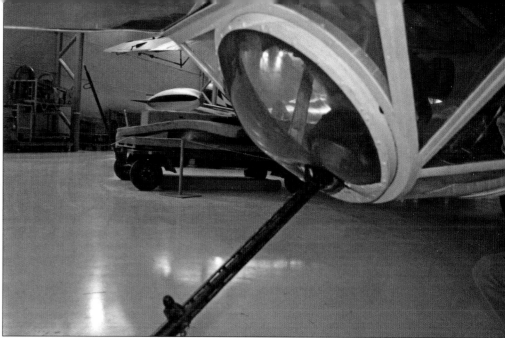

Two rows of Plexiglas windows are located on the gondola sides and the lower fuselage directly above. The gunner's vision is laterally enhanced by the insertion of large Plexiglas side panels. The trailing aerial fairlead is slightly angled outwards, and the aerial wire has a black weight on the end.

Access to the aircraft's interior is through a hatch located in the center of the gondola. The hatch is hinged on the port side and is photographed in the open position.

The rear-mounted MG 15 on the He 111P-2 is inserted into a circular Plexiglas frame that rotates in the same manner as the Ikaria unit in the nose of the cockpit. However, unlike the Ikaria fitting, the Plexiglas surface is unobstructed by cross frames.

A full side view of the starboard side of the gondola emphasises its relatively neat outline. The trailing aerial fairlead feeds out of the fuselage through the second Plexiglas panel from the front. It is vertically and outwardly-aligned to the fuselage.

The large black handle on the circular Plexiglas frame allows the Bordschütze (Gunner) to rotate it. The spent cartridge cases were discovered in the gondola when the He 111-P was recovered for restoration.

A view of the gondola's port side demonstrates how access to the aircraft was not easy when wearing bulky flight gear, given the fuselage's close proximity to the ground at this point. The camouflage separation line has been neatly applied.

Late Tail Cone

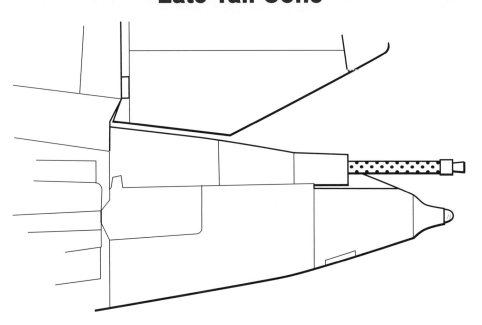

Glider Hook Installation

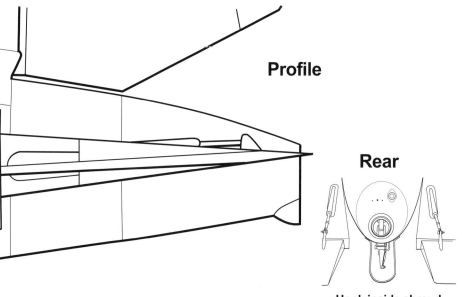

Profile

Rear

Hook inside shroud

A large square Plexiglas panel is positioned in the base of the fuselage directly behind the rear of the gondola. This was another regular feature fitted to all variants of the He 111P and H Models.

The Lorenz blind-landing beam aerials are positioned under the rear fuselage. There are two separate units with the larger one at the front. The power leads feed into two circular fittings placed between the units. The rear aerial length is normally the same as the forward aerial with three supports.

A fuller view from the side shows the triangular arrangement of the forward landing gear supports. The bracket at the bottom right forms the main break-point upon the gear's retraction. The lower strut linking the bracket and wheel-strut folds forwards.

The He 111's main landing gear consists of two struts enclosing the wheel. An X-pattern bracing frame is positioned between the struts. Also seen is the distinctive cross-ribbing on the wheel surface. The struts' overall color is gray but the metal oleo units towards the bottom are silver. The landing gear retracts backwards.

A view of the landing gear wheel picks out the left axle mounting, and the towing ring attached to the axle's front. White lettering advises that all air pressure be bled before detaching the wheel. Red lettering recommends a maximum air pressure of 3.2 Atus. The red air-brake leads change to Black in between the oleo and wheel-hub.

Landing Gear

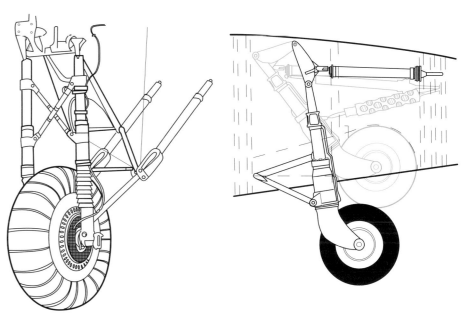

This angle view demonstrates how the main retraction brackets also form the front section of the rear support rods. The cross-braced struts above the brackets swivel backwards, while the solid "yoke" casting to which they in turn are linked folds up into the nacelle roof.

The landing gear's rear support struts are secured within channels cut into front of the rear wing-spar. The apparent imbalance in the struts' height is due to the engine-nacelles being fitted in line with the outer-wing dihedral angle rather than the horizontal inner-wing structure.

A gear locking mechanism with a lever and wire is normally mounted at the inner bracket-end as seen here on the CAF's He 111. The cable extends up to a pulley mounted on the bay's side-wall. The He 111P-2 lacks this equipment at present.

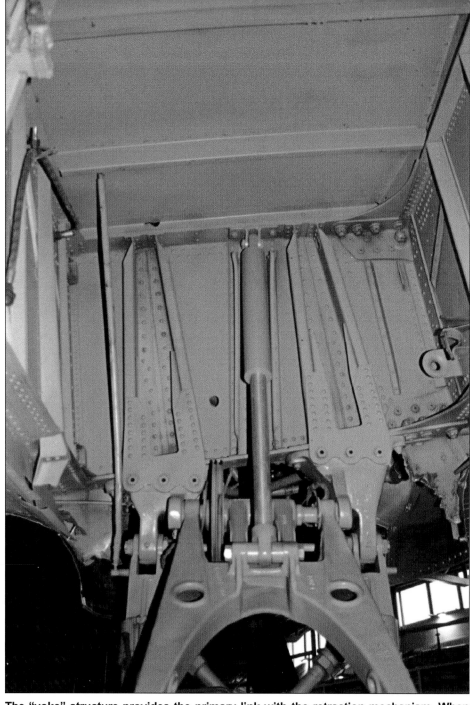

A forward view demonstrates how the lower struts are attached within the bracket-ends, while the cross-braced frame has its link-points on the inside surfaces of the brackets. The solid nature of the "yoke" structure is evident from this angle.

The "yoke" structure provides the primary link with the retraction mechanism. When retraction is completed the retraction rod is fully enclosed within its "sheath." The exact function of the thin rod attached to the left wheel strut is unclear.

The wheel-struts' horizontal swivel rod is secured by nuts to the base of twin castings. The castings in turn are bolted to a horizontal beam and their facings secured at the front and back to U-pattern frames extending down from the top of the nacelle. The inner surfaces of the castings form the attachment-points for the retraction "yoke."

The great thickness of the He 111's wing structure is emphasized by this view of the starboard wheel bay. The gear locking cable pulley is normally positioned out from the top of the angular frame in the middle of the side-wall. This He 111P-2 totally lacks its landing gear doors.

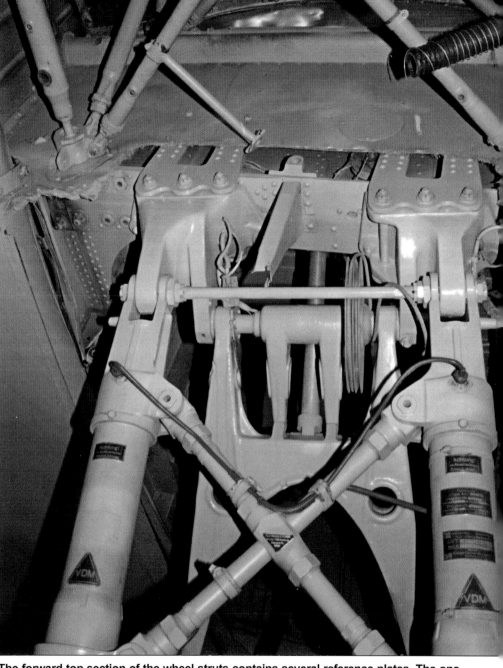

The forward top section of the wheel struts contains several reference plates. The one at the top right recommends the air pressure be drained prior to separating the various sections of the red-colored leads. The triangular plates with the letters VDM confirm the manufacturer of the landing gear as Vereinigte Deutsche Metallwerke, which also provided the P-2's propellers.

45

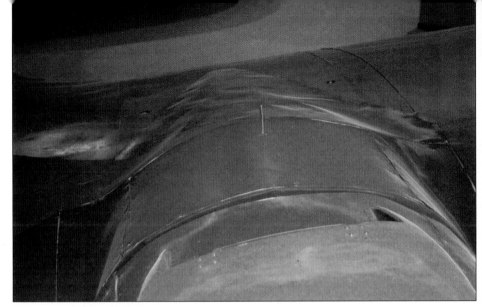

The rear cowling panel on the top surface normally features a series of louvers that direct cooling air onto the oil tank. These have also been excluded during restoration. The broad metal strip covering the inner/outer wing joint is seen on the right.

He 111 H-22 with Fi 103 (V1)

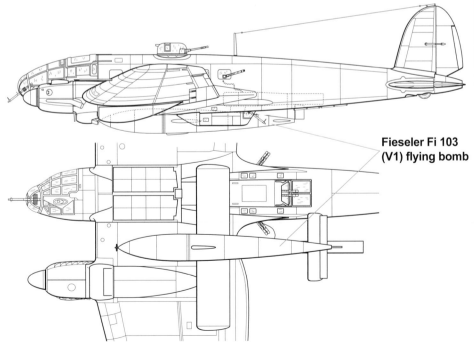

Fieseler Fi 103 (V1) flying bomb

Head-on view of the engine cowling picks out the oil cooler air-intake grill under its fairing, the supercharger cover on the port side of the cowling and the line of angled-down exhaust stubs. The VDM logo has a Black background.

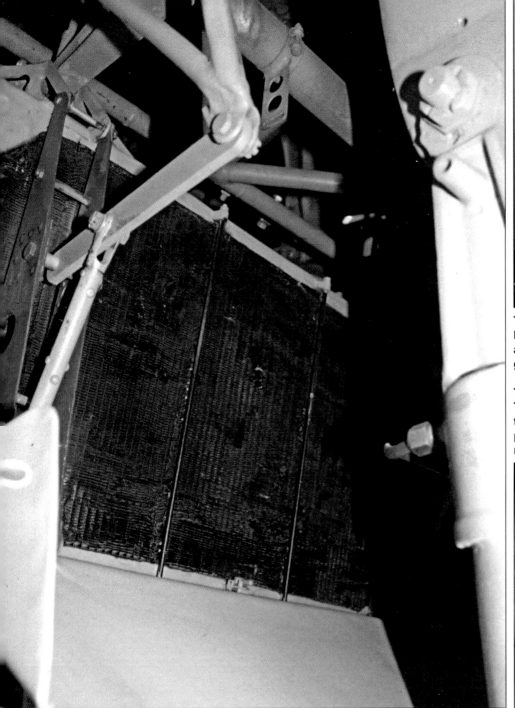

The DB 601A-1's radiators positioned below and to the rear of the engine block are housed in large fairings. Both are in the lowered position; when raised they present a smaller frontage that provides less airflow resistance in flight. The reference to the glycol content is applied in large red letters.

This is an example of the SC250, the heaviest bomb the He 111 could carry internally. The SC (Sprengbombe-Cylindrisch) denotes a thin-cased general-purpose missile in this case. The Yellow stripe at the end confirms the weapon's SC status. The SC250 is painted Gray-Green. The other two SC250s appear to be cement practice bombs; the nearside one appears to have a fuse socket despite its inert function!

The radiator flap is seen in the lowered position to provide a view of the radiator's rear mesh screen. The flap's movements are controlled by two linked supports.

The small missile resting against the cement SC250 seems to be a larger version of the trio in the foreground. Their size denotes an incendiary function. However, the solid 'plug' in the larger example's nose suggests a similar practice duty to the cement SC250.

The aerial torpedo (Luft-torpedo) LT F5b alongside the He 111P-2 is mounted on its lifting cradle. The 'scissors' frames expand to place the torpedo against the bomber's undersides. It is then attached to either an ETC2000 or PVC1006 pylon, two of which are positioned over one or both of the bomb-bay doors.

The mobile auxiliary starter unit is mounted within a cradle, whose lower tubular frame ends in a V-pattern with a vertical support at the end. The equipment's color appears to accord to a light shiny Brown. Red markings on Gray bomb-fin on the left indicate attachment to semi-armor piercing SD (Sprengbombe-Dickwandig) bombs.

Another standard Luftwaffe piece of support equipment was the mobile oil-tank trailer. Three adjustable rod-braces in a triangular configuration hold the trailer upright when detached from its towing vehicle. The overall color is believed to be a mix of RLM75 Gray and RLM76 Light Gray.

He 111H-6 Specifications

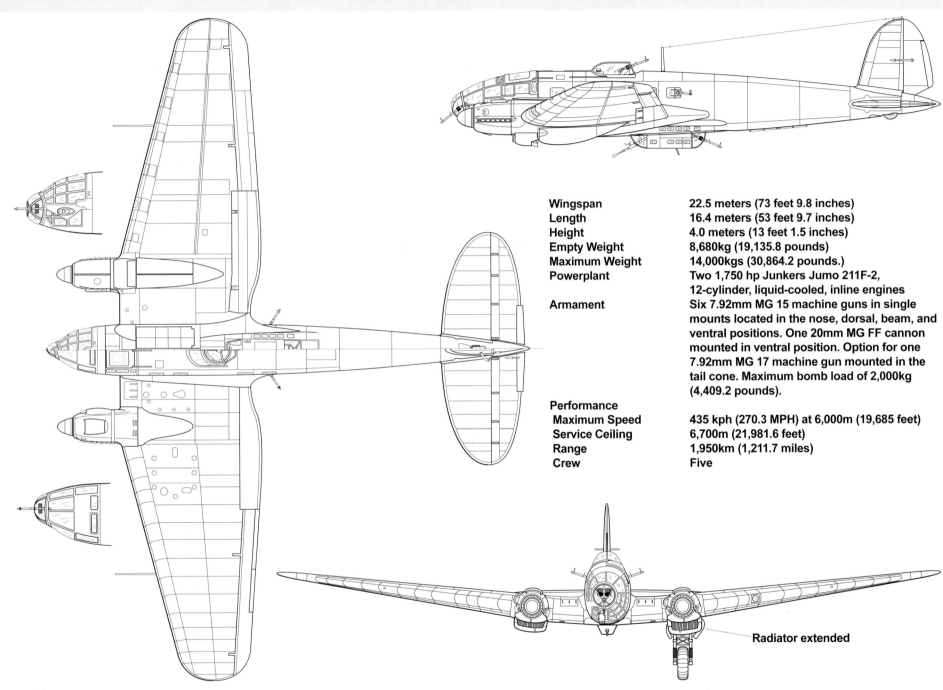

Wingspan	22.5 meters (73 feet 9.8 inches)
Length	16.4 meters (53 feet 9.7 inches)
Height	4.0 meters (13 feet 1.5 inches)
Empty Weight	8,680kg (19,135.8 pounds)
Maximum Weight	14,000kgs (30,864.2 pounds.)
Powerplant	Two 1,750 hp Junkers Jumo 211F-2, 12-cylinder, liquid-cooled, inline engines
Armament	Six 7.92mm MG 15 machine guns in single mounts located in the nose, dorsal, beam, and ventral positions. One 20mm MG FF cannon mounted in ventral position. Option for one 7.92mm MG 17 machine gun mounted in the tail cone. Maximum bomb load of 2,000kg (4,409.2 pounds).

Performance	
Maximum Speed	435 kph (270.3 MPH) at 6,000m (19,685 feet)
Service Ceiling	6,700m (21,981.6 feet)
Range	1,950km (1,211.7 miles)
Crew	Five

Radiator extended

He 111H-20 Specifications

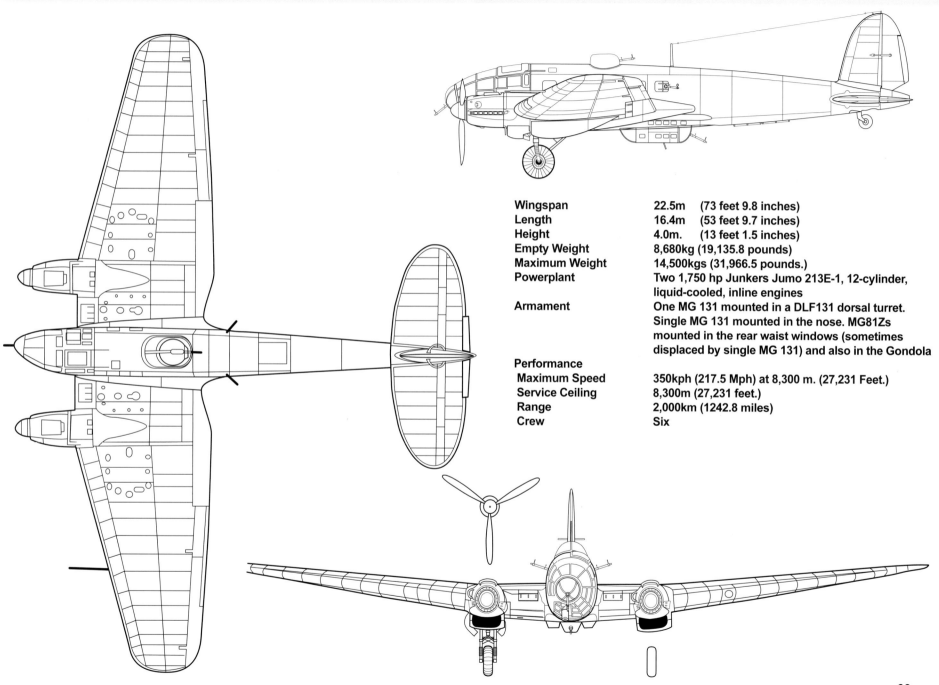

Wingspan	22.5m (73 feet 9.8 inches)
Length	16.4m (53 feet 9.7 inches)
Height	4.0m. (13 feet 1.5 inches)
Empty Weight	8,680kg (19,135.8 pounds)
Maximum Weight	14,500kgs (31,966.5 pounds.)
Powerplant	Two 1,750 hp Junkers Jumo 213E-1, 12-cylinder, liquid-cooled, inline engines
Armament	One MG 131 mounted in a DLF131 dorsal turret. Single MG 131 mounted in the nose. MG81Zs mounted in the rear waist windows (sometimes displaced by single MG 131) and also in the Gondola

Performance

Maximum Speed	350kph (217.5 Mph) at 8,300 m. (27,231 Feet.)
Service Ceiling	8,300m (27,231 feet.)
Range	2,000km (1242.8 miles)
Crew	Six

The RAF Museum's example of the Günter brothers' design is a transport variant with the official designation He 111-20/R1 but converted to H-23 standard. It was handed over to the 56FG at the end of WWII, following its reported rejection on grounds of its over-scale proportions for shipment to, and test evaluation in, the USA.

The circular and rotating Ikaria mounting carried by He 111 bombers has been fitted with the square plate that was a feature on variants from the He 111-10, onward. It normally carried an aperture for a machine-gun or cannon-caliber weapon but this has been blanked out.

A close-up shot of the portable fire-extinguisher shows the shaped carrying frame secured to the container-top and the triangular hose nozzle with its fluted outlet.. The extinguisher contains carbonic acid, confirmed by the word *Kohlensäure* stencilled on the upper section.

The starboard-rear section of the He 111's cockpit features a large Plexiglas panel that hinges downwards and serves as an escape hatch in an emergency. The panel access lever is sprayed red as a visual warning for crewmembers to operate it only when this is deemed necessary.

The radio-mast on the H-20 is located just beyond the rear side-window. It is parallel-sided with an L-shaped top, and the black antenna-wire mounting is secured at this point. The wire extends horizontally from the upper fin to the mast, then traces vertically into the fuselage.

The He 111's fuselage features two pairs of square-edged windows on both sides. The plate fitted to the rear window is thought to blank off the original mount for a machine-gun. The raised panel ahead of the radio-mast closes off the aperture for the Drehlafette (DLF) turret. The flexible frame for the gondola lies in the foreground.

A second view of the gondola demonstrates the large aperture that is created by the hatch being opened (or, in this case, detached). The generous dimensions of the space are necessary to ensure a safe exit for the paratrooper contingent.

The standard underside gondola on the He 111 normally has an entrance hatch in the center. In this H-20/R1 variation, the rear section in the foreground swings up into the fuselage along with the Plexiglas panel located in the fuselage just behind the gondola.

The gondola on the Commemorative Air Force's Casa-He111 has the same overall outline as the H-22. However, during WWII the small Plexiglas panels on the lower fuselage were reduced to the two at either end from the He111H-20 onwards. The blanked-off frontal strip was another standard feature first introduced on the H-16 variant.

The frontal area of the gondola on He 111 remained un-glazed on the H-1 and on the great majority of H-16 to H-22 variants. The Plexiglas frame has been applied to the Hendon aircraft but a plate appears to cover the slot in which armament could be inserted.

The Lorenz blind-landing aerial is seen in its standard location on the He 111. However, a sheath has been placed over the fitting in this instance.

A basic modification on the Hendon He 111H-20 was the deletion of the bomb-bay equipment and bomb doors. In their place was fitted a rectangular platform with attachment points that permitted the external carriage of equipment containers or other supplies.

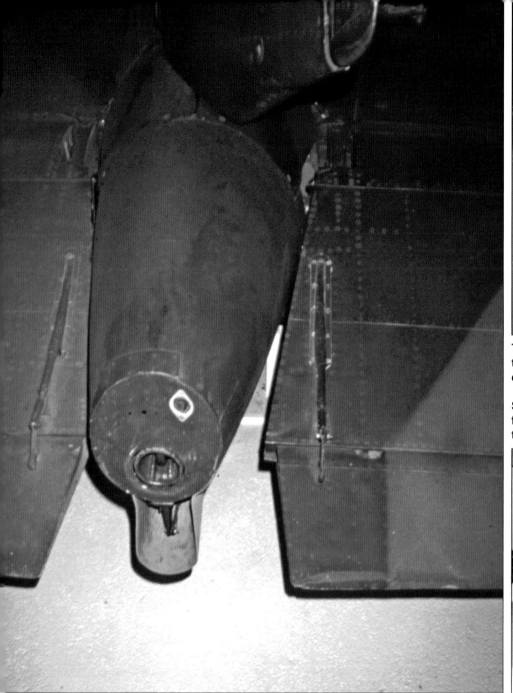

The control rods for the elevator trim-tabs are similar in pattern to the unit fitted to the rudder. Their forward sections are channelled into metal sheaths attached to the elevator surface.

Small panels are located directly under the rudder base where it meets with the rear fuselage. These provide access to the elevators' central mechanism. Four screws hold the panels in place. Also visible are the rudder and elevator trim-tab control rods.

View of the He 111H-20's tail cone picks out the mount at its base, which houses the attachment-point for glider towing-ropes or wires. Directly below the cone is the scoop forming the outlet for the fuel-jettison system.

The pilot's foot pedals are almost vertically aligned, and are mounted on support frames. The frame and lightening slits in the rear section have a different overall shape from those on the He 111P-2's pedals. Also on view is the brake cylinder, which is shorter and greater in diameter compared to the He 111P-2 units.

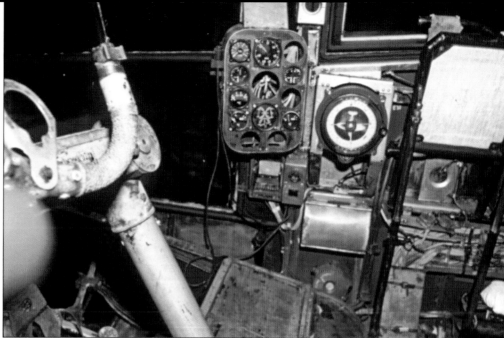

The He 111H-20 variant has a back-up instrument panel located in front of the radio-compass. The panel lacks the facings or instrumentation to half the dials. The automatic-pilot turn-switch that activates the rudder only is seen in the foreground; it is mounted on the top of the pilot's right hand-grip.

Engine Exhaust Development

He 111H-10 through H-16

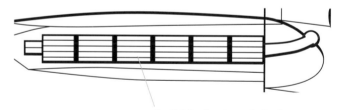

Individual exhaust stacks

He 111H-16 through H-23

Exhaust flame damper

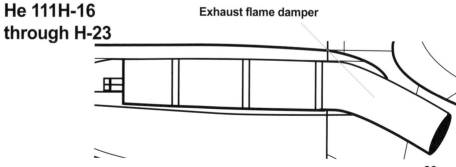

Looking forward in the passenger compartment. The benches for as many as 16 paratroopers are covered in mid-green colored material, while the foot-rests appear to be metal with diamond-pattern surfaces.

The rear section of the H-20's fuselage interior is left in anodised metal. Control pulleys (center) and push/pull control rods (bottom) trace along the port side. The frame with oval aperture in the background is the fuselage / tail-plane mounting unit. The master-compass normally sits just inside the access hatch and on the port side floor.

A second picture taken in the passenger compartment shows the interior of the gondola. The gondola's flexible section that swings up into the fuselage has been detached.

The oxygen supply and control unit for the passenger compartment is mounted in the rear section of the passenger compartment roof.

The DFL131 rotating turret borne by this He 111 variant has been detached and a square fairing placed over the external fuselage surface. The circular aperture for the turret mount is spanned by two beams and is fringed by a hexagonal frame.

Closer view of the unit picks out the oxygen-pressure gauge on the left. The circular-shaped main control bears the words Sauerstoff-Dusche that translates as "Oxygen-Spray."

71

The aileron hinges are located within narrow recesses built into the wing surface. The small pipe mounted in this position on either wing serves as an overflow vent for the outer fuel tank, and was introduced on later variants of the He 111H.

With the flaps in the lowered position, the port aileron's end surface is exposed. This view shows how the inner tab has been adjusted in relation to the aileron's situation. Also apparent is the concave rear edge of the aileron into which the tab's leading edge slots. The trim-tabs also operate in conjunction with the flaps to provide extra lift.

The control surface has been moved upwards, exposing the leading edge of the port aileron's inner set-back hinge's and the large lightening hole in its center.

The port outer wing section on the He 111H-20 has been detached. The separation line with the inner section is alongside the engine nacelle. The pipe is believed to feed hot air to the wing leading-edges to prevent the surfaces from icing-up. The landing-gear door is the standard He 111 pattern. There is an H-20 reference below the pipe and there are four wing-attachment points at the frame corners.

The area around the fuel tank located between the engine and fuselage features a series of seven circular access panels that vary in diameter.

The mass-balance for the rudder takes the shape of a curved forward section mounted on the fin. A straight rod at the section's end that is mounted on the forward edge of the rudder completes the fitting. The overall shape is similar to that on the He 111 P-2 but lacks the triangular fairing over the rudder-end that was fitted to the P-2.

Three small access holes on the outer wing surface are positioned on the fuel tank access panel. The larger example further back borders the metal strip-fairing that covers the break line between the inner and outer wing sections.

The removal of the propeller spinner cover reveals the securing collars of the three blades. Each blade has a threaded base that secures it in place within the hub. The propeller-blade feathering mechanism is housed in the black unit.

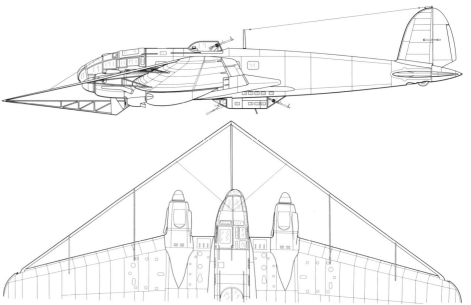

He 111H-8 cable cutter installation

Alternate cable cutter installation

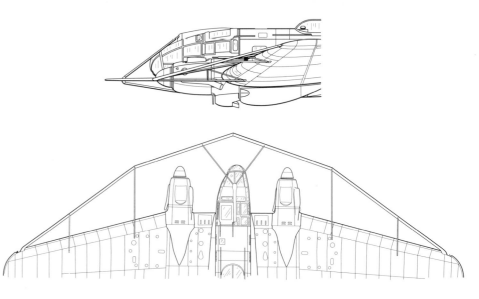

The He 111H20/R-1's propeller is of the VS11 type. It is manufactured from wood and features broader blades and a marginally larger-diameter spinner cover than the VDM airscrews have. The design replaced the VDM-manufactured units from the He 111H-6 onwards. The blades are finished in RLM71 Dark Green.

This view of the underside of the port Jumo motor reveals the white-colored pipes on either side of the panel-securing strips that act as cooling-air ducts. The exhaust stub covers are the standard pattern introduced from the He 111P onwards.

The port radiator bath is exposed and displays its rectangular frame as well as the mesh screen. The three screws at the bottom of the frame link up with holes in the base of the radiator fairing when this is in place.

The port engine on the RAF Museum's He 111 is uncovered along its lower surface. The holes drilled into the fixed frames form the cowling panels' securing points. Also seen at the top is the bulged shape of the supercharger air-intake.

The engine bearer-frame is seen at the top of the engine mass. The circular shapes at the front and towards the end of the frame accommodate the anti-vibration rubber pads.

The main bearer frame is supported by a secondary arm extending down from the rear anti-vibration unit. The rectangular tubular structure to which the bearer frame and secondary arm are attached can be seen directly above the radiator bath.

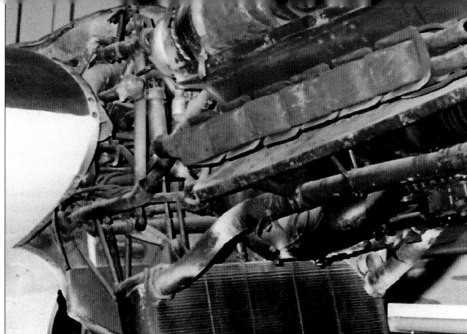

Two pipes lead from the top corners of the radiator bath. Here the left-hand pipe has been disconnected. The radiator is secured to the rectangular frame above by thin metal rods.

Engine Nacelle Development

He 111H-10 through H-16

He 111H-16 through H-23

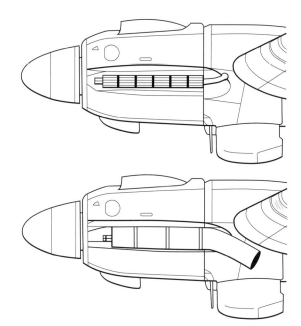

The engine's fuel injector unit is located directly below the center of the engine block. The exhaust stubs are placed within a curved metal trough. The red discoloration is due to liberal application of preservative material.

Towards the left of this view from directly below the port engine is a large black pipe that is part of the engine compression system. Directly behind the propeller/cowling junction is a frame attached to the engine block front that is perforated by a series of large holes that permit access of cooling air to the engine mass.

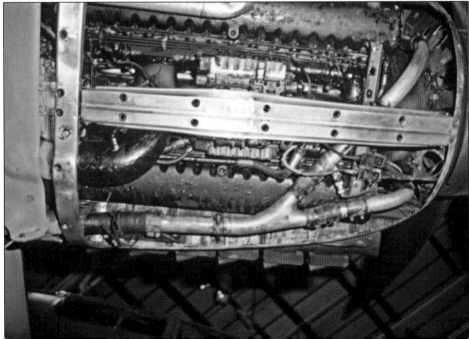

This angle view of the frontal cowling directly behind the propeller base-plate shows the series of teardrop apertures that allow cooling air onto the engine block. Removal of the engine supercharger cover shows its large diameter and position adjacent to the engine bearer frame.

77

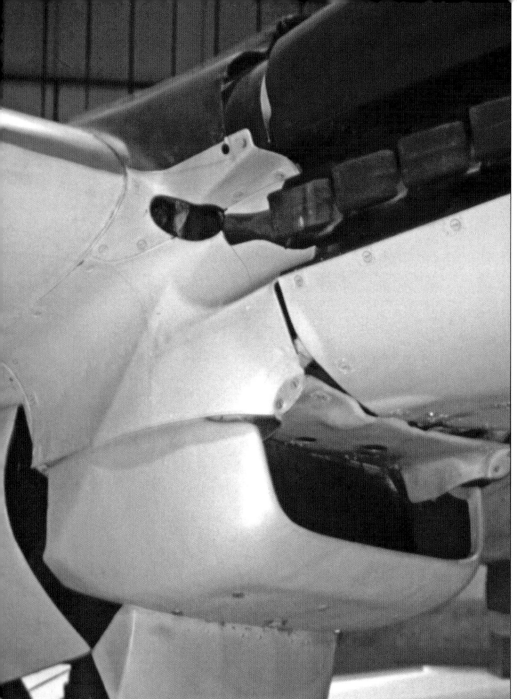

The engine oil-cooler is located on the forward section of the engine block and is covered by a bulged panel. The panel surface features raised rows of screws on its central surface compared to the bulk of the cowling screws that are flush-fitted.

The Jumo's oil tank is positioned on the top of the engine cowling. The holes on the right of the picture form the ends of twin rows of cooling louvers for the tank that is mounted directly below.

The He 111H's rear exhaust stubs are extended over pipe units with a single expanded orifice at the rear. These direct the exhaust into the wings through oval apertures positioned on the nacelle edges as seen here.

This flight of He 111P-1 bombers is in the air at around the onset of WWII. The visible code E33 on the bomber in the foreground indicates attachment to KG255. The D/F loop (Peil EP) on the rear fuselage was replaced on the P-2 variant by Peil G5 equipment positioned within the dorsal turret canopy.

The Beobachter's forward position is seen here with the bomb-sight detached from the oval bracket mounting in the center. Two small dials at the front provide airspeed (L) and altitude information. Ammunition drum bracket is mounted along the frame's right-side.

The pilot's seat from a He 111 is seen attached to what appears to be a test-board. The bellows mechanism's link-up to the tubular frame is also depicted. The two knurled wheels at either side of the frame are (L) the rudder trim-control and (R) the aileron trim-control.

79

He 111P-2 - 1939

On 26 October 1939 KG26 'Löwen' (Lion) attacked naval shipping in the Firth of Forth, Scotland. This He 111P-2 of the Geschwader Stab.was downed south of Edinburgh by RAF fighters to become the first German aircraft since WWI to descend on British soil.

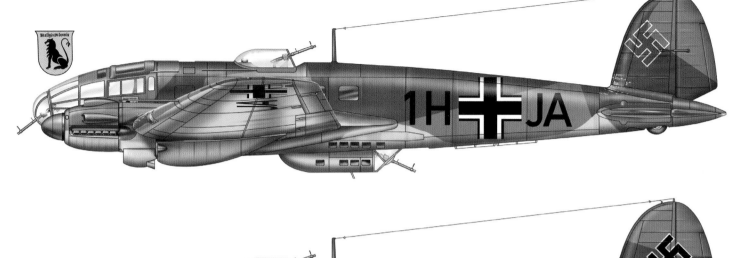

He 111P-2

KG54 bore the title 'Totenkopf" (Deaths Head). Only I and II Gruppen operated on the He 111 at the outbreak of WWII and the Geschwader converted to the Ju88 during the 1939/40 period. The bomber depicted here was assigned to 2 Staffel.

He111P-2

Many Luftwaffe bombers had their camouflage and markings dulled-down during the Blitz upon Britain in 1940/41. The matt black application helped to absorb the worst of the searchlight batteries' effect. This He111P-2 belongs to KG55 'Greif' (Griffen).

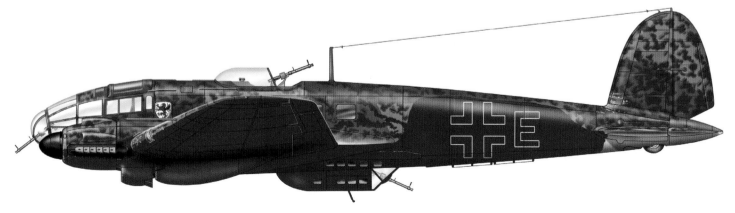

He111H-3

K.Gr. (Kampfgruppe) 100 was a specialist unit tasked with introducing the blind-bombing device 'X-Gerät' into operational service during the 1940/41 Blitz on Britain. The He111H-3 seen here flew with 2 Staffel.

He111H-8

(Balloon-cutting frame)
Thirty He111H-3 and H-5 aircraft were converted to bear heavy balloon cable-cutting frames. Categorised as He111H-8s, the lack of success coupled with sharply reduced operational performance caused the frames to be removed, and the surviving aircraft were re-assigned to glider-towing duties.

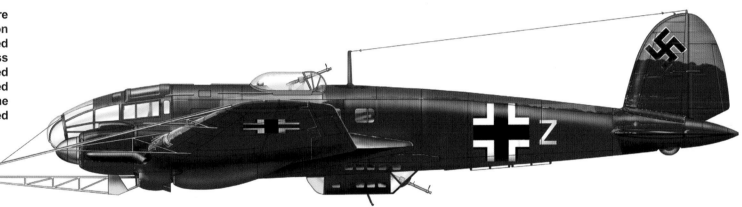

He111H-6 - Russia

The Luftwaffe camouflaged their aircraft according to the season, in this case winter. White soluble distemper that could easily be washed off was crudely applied to the aircraft's surfaces. This He111H-6 belongs to 6/KG53 'Condor Legion' operating on the Russian Front in 1941/42. Markings are restricted to the yellow aircraft letter. Yellow wingtip under-sides denote service on the Eastern front.

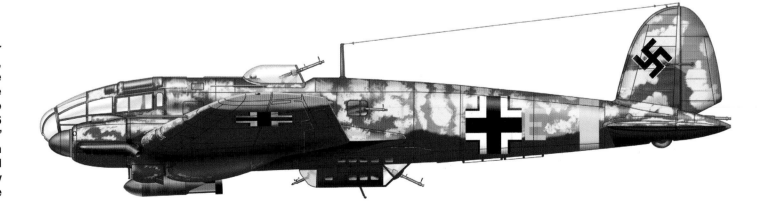

The KG26 He 111H in this picture has probably been force-landed onto a sandy shoreline, to judge by the thoroughly plastered fuselage surface. Detachment of the rudder and removal of the fairings around the tail section indicate the bomber will be stripped down ready for transport. Details of the incident are not to hand.

A He 111P from KG55 amply demonstrates the switch from normal camouflage patterns to one that is "dulled down" for nocturnal operations during the 1940-1941 "Blitz." Black paint is applied to all wing and stabilizer surfaces and rear fuselage sides up to the end of the wing fillets. A speckled pattern is also applied to the remaining fuselage area.

This He 111P belongs to the GeschwaderStab of KG55, based at Villacoublay near Paris during the Battle of Britain. The rough grass surface gives a false impression of the airfield facilities since proper runway facilities were available there.

The temporary winter camouflage scheme on the upper surfaces of this KG55 He 111P operating on the Eastern Front is badly eroded. The fully-enclosed dorsal turret provides the gunner with freedom from exposure to the particularly harsh Russian weather. The single SC1000 slung externally seems a minimal load although the starboard bomb bay is available for the stowage of up to 1,000kgs.

The He 111P's withdrawal from front-line operations saw its use in secondary duties. This example is serving in a diplomatic role around late 1942. Records indicate that the Heinkel He 111P-2 with the designation D-APOW was used by the Waffenstillstandskommission ("Armistice Commission") that monitored the Franco-German armistice of 1940.

Le Bourget within Paris was home for II/KG55 during the Battle of Britain. A He 111P-2 (G1+BP) displays yellow propeller spinners to denote its assignment to the Gruppe's third Staffel. The absence of proper surfaced dispersals was typical for this period of Luftwaffe operations.

One of the 11 losses borne by the Luftwaffe on 10/11 May 1941 involved an He 111H-5 from 5/KG53 flown by Ltn. Richard Furthmann. He and the other three crew members were fortunate to survive the crash-landing that stopped right up against the solid tree-line and smashed the nose Plexiglas. The black distemper has obliterated all fuselage markings.

The innate structural integrity of the He 111 is demonstrated in this picture. A flak burst has severely mangled the starboard stabilizer and liberally peppered the rear fuselage; despite this, the pilot was able to maintain flight and land his machine.

He111H-6

He111's were regularly utilised as personal transports for Senior military staff. The He111H-6 seen here served in this capacity for Gen. Erwin Rommel in the Mediterranean Theater of Operations during 1941.

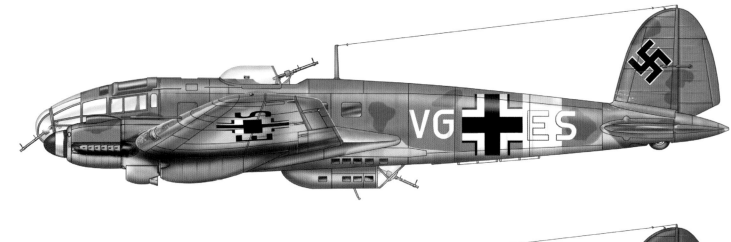

He111H-6
(Captured aircraft)

No. 260 Sqdn (RAF) claimed this He111H-6 assigned to KG4 that was found abandoned on Castel Beneto airfield near Tripoli, Libya, in North Africa around December 1942. It was still airworthy and was used as a 'hack' by the Sqdn personnel.

He111H-16

The white soluble distemper finish applied to this He111H-16 would not long survive front line operations. The 2/KG27 aircraft was operating on the Eastern Front during the winter of 1942/43.

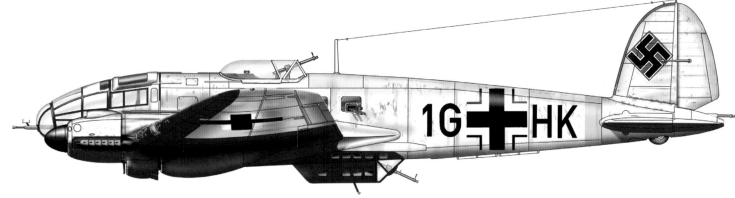

He111H-16 (Spanish)

The Spanish Air Force was provided with a number of He111H-16s during WWII, and Spain's aviation constructors CASA also assembled a further number under licence. The lack of Jumo engines after 1945 was equalised by the purchase of Rolls-Royce Merlins and total conversion of the He111 fleet was completed by the mid-1950s.

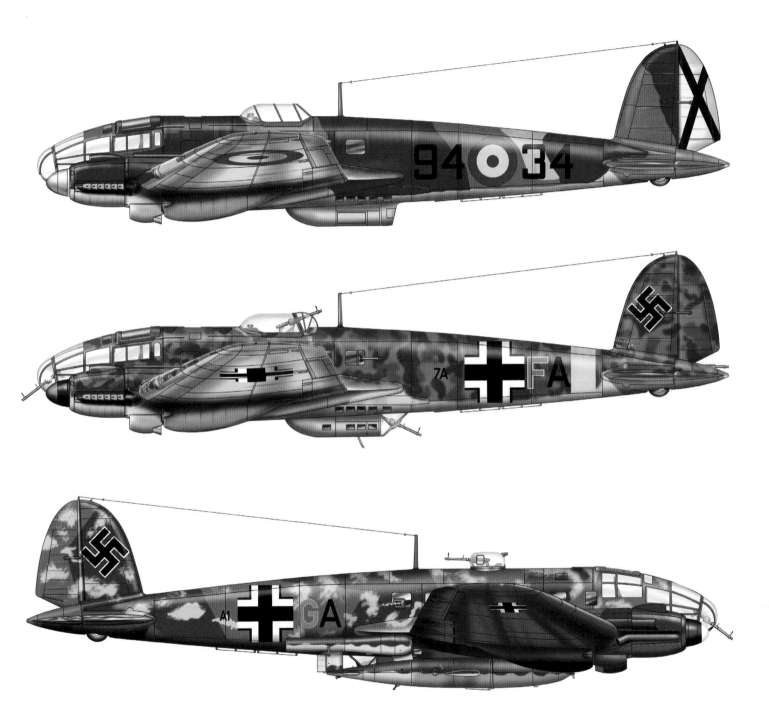

He111H-6

Finland was an Axis co-partner along with Nazi Germany in the struggle against the Soviet Union. The He111H-6 depicted here belongs to the Staff Flight of Gefechtsverband Kuhlmey that was operating out of Immola in Finland during July 1944. Yellow fuselage and wing-tip bands confirm that the unit is based on the Eastern Front.

He111H-22

Launched in the winter of 1944-1945, Operation "Rumpelkammer" involved the air-launch of the infamous V-1 "Doodle-bug" against the British mainland. This He111H-22 of Geschwaderstab/KG53 was based at Venlo, Holland.

On 9 December 1944 this He 111H landed at San Severo, Italy, occupied by the 31FG. The rear view picks out the fully enclosed dorsal canopy introduced on the H-16 variant. A beam-mounted weapon is located in the rear fuselage window. The forward pairs of fuselage windows feature small circular Plexiglas inserts, which are believed to be an adaptation introduced on the H-10 or H-11 variant.

A frontal view of the same He 111 reveals the 20mm MG FF cannon in the nose and the spiral markings on the propeller spinners. On board were seven Hungarian military personnel and family members whose intention was to desert to the Allied Cause.

A snow-covered airfield on the Eastern front forms the background for an He 111H unit. The row of SC50 bombs have tubes fitted to their X-pattern vanes; the slipstream filtering through these produced the screaming note primarily associated with Luftwaffe ordnance used in World War II.

This He 111H is seen following the airfield's occupation by U.S. troops in May 1945. The extra aerial directly behind the cockpit is a clear indication that the bomber is or was equipped with the Y Gerät blind-bombing and navigation system. The aircraft is fitted with the later-pattern ventral gondola.

Dorsal Armament Development

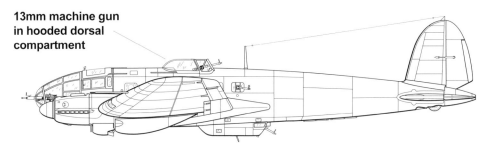

13mm machine gun in hooded dorsal compartment

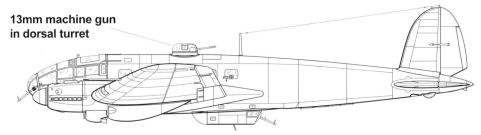

13mm machine gun in dorsal turret

Nose Armament Development

He 111H-16

20mm MG FF cannon, with L-FF/6 sight mounted atop weapon

He 111H-20 through H-23

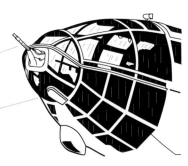

13mm MG 131 machine gun

Spent cartridge port

This is the Drehlafette (DLF) rotating turret first mounted in He 111H-16 airframes. The gunner has a good all-round field of view thanks to the frameless Plexiglas cover. There is a small Plexiglas insert in the forward fuselage window. The puppy's obvious apprehension at facing a long drop to earth lends an incongruous air to the picture.

This picture of an airworthy He 111 could have been mistaken for one taken during WWII but for the Rolls-Royce Merlins that replace the standard Jumo or DB power-plants. Sadly, the former Spanish Air Force aircraft that was acquired by the CAF's Arizona Wing suffered a fatal crash in July 2003. There are currently no airworthy He 111s. (Rich Kolasa)